CYCLELOG

Diary and Guide for the Cyclist
Fourth Edition

Tim Houts
Jan Bass

NTC/Contemporary Publishing Group

Published by Masters Press
A division of NTC/Contemporary Publishing Group, Inc.
4255 West Touhy Avenue, Lincolnwood (Chicago), Illinois 60646-1975 U.S.A.
Copyright © 1993 by Sports Log Publishers
All rights reserved. No part of this book may be reproduced, stored in a retrieval system, or transmitted in any form or by any means, electronic, mechanical, photocopying, recording, or otherwise, without the prior permission of NTC/Contemporary Publishing Group, Inc.
Printed in the United States of America
International Standard Book Number: 1-57028-057-6

18 17 16 15 14 13 12 11 10 9 8 7 6 5 4 3 2

Introduction and Preface to the Fourth Edition

Introduction
Welcome to CycleLog.

We created CycleLog to be the ultimate training diary, with all the features cyclists want. CycleLog offers more room to record your training than any diary available, plus concise and helpful training tips and workouts. Our full-color and black-and-white photos offer motivation and inspiration throughout the training year.

Note your training plateaus, valleys and peaks in the diary. Use the training information in the guide to bring you faster times and increased performance. And enjoy the photos featured throughout the book.

Preface to the Fourth Edition
First, thank you for making CycleLog so successful! Thanks to your great support and suggestions we've sold out of three printings and are now in our fourth edition. Second, here's a recap of CycleLog features:

Easy to use diary
You'll quickly appreciate our diary layout. You'll see a full week of training spread over facing pages. And, most importantly, you'll have plenty of room to write. CycleLog has more flexibility and room to write than any diary available.

56 weeks of diary pages
CycleLog offers the most number of pages to record your training, giving you 56 weeks of undated diary pages to record your training. And because they are undated, you can start and stop using the diary according to your schedule.

24 ALL NEW photographs
This edition features 24 ALL NEW full-color and black-and-white photographs to inspire and motivate throughout your training year. Enjoy them!

Good luck on a great season of training and racing.

Jan Bass and Tim Houts

Log Your Best

Give yourself or a friend the best training diaries available!
Masters Press' SportsLog Series is your training accessory partner with its full line of training diaries. Feel free to tell a friend or a training partner about our products and call or write us for more information or to reorder any SportsLog title.

The SportsLog Series includes:
RunLog   **LiftLog**
WalkLog   **TriLog**
CycleLog   **SwimLog**

Call (800)9-SPORTS to order!
Call toll-free in the U.S. or call (317) 298-5706 from outside the U.S. or write: Masters Press, 2647 Waterfront Pkwy. E. Drive, Suite 100, Indianapolis, IN 46214. Good luck with your training!

About the Authors

Jan Bass

Jan Bass has trained and raced extensively in his 15 years as a cycling Category 2 road racer. Coaching seven cycling and triathlete teams to successful seasons, Jan founded and developed an innovative and leading bicycle/triathlon retail store in Los Angeles. Jan is currently training with punishing training rides in Northern California.

Tim Houts

Tim is the author of several fitness books. With more than 200,000 copies in print, the books cover a variety of sports and activities, including walking, running, cycling and weight lifting.

Tim began participating in competitive athletics at the age of nine, enjoying the camaraderie and competition of his local age-group swim team. He went on to play water polo at Stanford University and then took up running after graduation. He has run numerous 10K's and three marathons. His interest in running and swimming has also led him to compete in many triathlons.

Today, Tim enjoys mixing his workouts to include fitness walking, running, swimming, mountain biking, and competing in an occasional 10K or open-water swimming event.

Credits:

All photographs © 1997 Jim Safford/Photosport
Cover design by Suzanne Lincoln
Book design by Heidi Sandison

Table of Contents

Part I: TRAINING GUIDE

Stretching	1
Nutrition	2
Map Your Goals	4
Building Endurance	5
Training for Power	6
Intervals	8
Fun Ones	10
Overtraining	11
Surviving Injuries	12
Other Books to Read	14
Getting More Out of Your Diary	15
How to Use Charts & Graphs	16
Goals Worksheet	17
Map to Raceday Worksheet	18
Race Results Summary	21
Cumulative Mileage Graph	23

Part II: TRAINING DIARY

Daily Diary Pages	25

Stretching

Stretching increases flexibility, improves your athletic performance and helps prevent injury. Stretch before and after each ride.

Stretch for flexibility

There are many ways to stretch your body, but the basics work the best:

Hurdler's Stretch

To stretch your hamstrings, sit on the floor with your right leg bent back, almost under your buttock. Place your left leg straight out in front. Slowly stretch your left leg by trying to touch your nose to your left knee. Never "bounce" to stretch. Hold the position for 30 seconds.

To stretch your quadriceps, from the same position, slowly lean your body back toward the point where your shoulders reach the floor. Hold for 30 seconds.

Switch right and left leg positions and repeat to stretch the right leg's hamstrings and the left leg's quadriceps.

Back and Hamstring Stretch

To stretch your hamstrings and your back, sit on the floor and place both legs straight in front, knees flat on the floor, toes pointed to the ceiling. Slowly bend at the waist and try to touch your nose to your knees. Hold for 30 seconds.

To stretch your back, while lying on your back, bring your right knee toward your chest and roll it over toward the floor next to your left arm. Hold for 15 seconds. Repeat with left knee.

Calf Stretch

To stretch your calf, stand facing a wall and place your palms against the wall, above your head. Place your right foot flat on the floor, away from the wall, while supporting yourself primarily on your bent left leg. Keep your right leg straight. Gently move your hips forward. Reverse right and left leg positions and repeat to stretch left calf.

Incorporate other muscle specific stretches as necessary. Get into the habit of stretching. A flexible body is less prone to injury, runs more smoothly and recovers faster.

Nutrition

Good, sound nutrition is a critical element to any training program. You want your body lean and well-fueled to train and race your best.

Remember these nutritional basics to keep your training on track:

Eat a balanced diet

A balanced diet includes: (1) carbohydrates, (2) proteins, (3) fats, and (4) vitamins and minerals.

Carbohydrates

Complex carbohydrates provide an excellent source of highly burnable "fuel" for training and racing, and often are a good source of protein, minerals and vitamins as well. Make carbohydrates 50-60% of your caloric intake.

Carbohydrates include: potatoes, rice, pasta, kasha, corn, peas, beans, and fruits and vegetables.

Proteins

Proteins provide a source to build and maintain strong bones and muscles. Make proteins 15% of your caloric intake.

Recent studies suggest that athletes in peak training may need up to 2 1/2 times the normal intake of protein to offset muscle breakdown. Adjust your protein intake to what works best for you.

Proteins include: meats, poultry, fish, cheese, beans and legumes (which are also carbohydrates), and whole-wheat grains.

Fats

Fats, in limited quantity, are important to your body make-up. However, fats (like cheese and salad oil) contain more than twice the calories, ounce-for-ounce, than protein or carbohydrates. Limit your fat intake to 25-30% of your total calories.

Fats include: butter, cheese, vegetable oils, fried foods, peanut butter, and olives.

Vitamins and minerals

Get all the vitamins and minerals you need in a well-balanced diet with plenty of fresh vegetables and fruits. Although all the vitamins and minerals needed by the human body can be found in a well balanced diet, consider vitamin supplements to offset deficiencies. Adjust your diet and supplements to what works best for you.

Limit sugars
Sugars like those in soft drinks and candy are empty calories which don't provide any nutritious value.

Limit sugars such as: chocolate, alcohol, hard candy, cake, cookies, pie, frozen yogurt, non-diet soft drinks, pancake syrup, jams, jellies, brown sugar, raw sugar, and foods containing sucrose or fructose.

Water is critical
When considering fluid replacement options during training efforts, remember that the most important element to replace during any ride is water. Water is critical to the body's cooling system. You'll become dehydrated if you don't replenish your body's water. Dehydration symptoms include: cramping, nausea, light-headedness, and fatigue to the point of collapse in extreme cases. None of these improve your finish place or time.

As a general rule, drink 4–6 ounces water every 15 minutes during a long ride or race. Adjust your water intake to the weather conditions and what works best for you.

Sports-drinks/bars help for long efforts
Your body will burn through your available blood sugar, or carbohydrates, in workouts or events longer than 1 1/2 – 2 hours. Take a sports-drink or energy bar as needed for events longer than 1 1/2 hours.

Check the label to see that the sports-drink you use contains no more than 5–10% sugar/carbohydrate (90–95% water) to maximize fluid absorption and prevent dehydration. Alternate drinks of water with sports–drinks to ensure adequate hydration. Find the sports drink/bar that works best for you. Take sports-drinks or bars on several training rides before you ever consider using it in a race. A race is the last place to find out how your body reacts to a particular beverage or bar.

Evaluate your diet
Track your diet for one week every six to nine months to see if your diet is made up of 55–60% carbohydrates, 15% proteins, and 25–30% fats. Adjust your diet accordingly based on the your results. Consider tracking your diet more frequently if you find it far off your goals.

Map Your Goals

Mapping goals—putting them on paper—will help you achieve objectives you already have in mind. Goals on paper, graphically displayed, offer a ready reference. Seeing where you started tells you where and how far you have to go.

Establish your starting point

Accurate goal-setting requires program-mapping. Review your current numbers: weight, personal-best times, best race placings, average weekly mileage, current training types—intervals, distance, or power.

Jot down important subjective information. Start by determining your level of commitment. List your overall energy-level, specific aches, pains, injuries, how you feel physically and emotionally upon finishing workouts or races, or other personal and pertinent observations.

Then, restate objectives and goals in a simple affirmative sentence. This could be a simple affirmation: "I'm committed to (achieving, accomplishing, bettering, doing) my performance-goal in/as (list the objective[s]). This serves as a self-contract.

Set attainable and measurable goals

Set goals as points to move toward from your current fitness levels—your starting point. Estimate how much time you'll need to reach your first increment. Maintain progress by setting smaller incremental goals. Use these as checkpoints. For example, knowing when you've reached your goal of riding 150 miles per week is easy. Knowing whether or not you've reached an un-measureable goal of "a good week of riding" is not.

Chart your training program

Having (1) determined your starting point, and (2) established reachable and measurable goals, you are now ready to goal-map to chart your fitness program. Use the Goals Worksheet and Map to Raceday Worksheet in this guide to list your goals and plan for a particular event.

Plan your program to prevent injury. Start slowly. Build slowly. Limit increases in mileage to no more than 10% per week. Be aware of influences in your work or personal life capable of affecting your training program.

Review and reward yourself

Review training efforts in comparison to goals every 30 to 90 days. Adjust your program as necessary. Break down a large goal into smaller segments if progress seems slow. Or revise your goals if your focus has changed.

Review and reward, rest and recreate yourself. Nobody else will. It's your responsibility. Enjoy an evening out. Sleep until noon one Saturday. Pat yourself on the shoulder and say: "Good work. Take a well-deserved break."

Building Endurance

Develop your cycling endurance base as the foundation for all other types of cycling training including intervals, power-work, and hills. Endurance is easy to build. It comes from spending enough time on the road and in the saddle. The big question is how much endurance do you need?

Set your distance

Look at your target event's length to determine how much endurance work you need. Mix in distances of up to 75%, 100% and 150% of the event distances. For example, do endurance rides building up to 38, 60, and 75 in preparation for a 50-mile event.

Limit speed or intensity work during your initial endurance building stage. Depending on your age and starting fitness level, this can be 1–2 months. Once you have a solid endurance base you can reduce your straight endurance work, since maintaining endurance conditioning takes less focus than building it.

Quality, not quantity

More is not necessarily better. Sometimes cyclists feel that by riding greater endurance training distances, almost to the point of punishment, they'll automatically become better and faster. All you'll get is slow legs, slower reaction time, and a lower top speed.

Don't waste energy overtraining in one area. Vary your workouts. Work in power rides, weight-training, speed-work, or training races. A couple of very long, easy-paced rides here and there never really hurt your overall training; but don't do longer, slower distance rides to the exclusion of higher quality, intensity training that puts the edge on your form.

Sample endurance workouts

Refer to this sample week of endurance workouts. The distances mentioned here are relative to your target event and to your conditioning as you move through your period of building endurance.:

Monday: *Long distance ride, easy*
Tuesday: *Medium ride*
Wednesday: *Cycling day off*
Thursday: *Short Ride*
Friday: *Cycling day off*
Saturday: *Long ride*
Sunday: *Medium ride*

Training for Power

Think of power as the ability to maintain momentum with short, focused efforts through tough spots on a ride. You use power to push through gusty winds, short hills, sudden accelerations, and rolling terrain.

Maintain momentum

Visualize power training rides as plain, hard, rides with extra focus on (1) maintaining momentum and (2) pedaling smoothly. When possible, ride with someone of equal or greater cycling fitness who will push you.

Begin your power ride by warming up as you ride to a familiar section of relatively uninterrupted road. Ease into your ride. Try to maintain a constant effort of about 85-95%. Use a heart-rate monitor, when available, to help you stay in your target range. In the absence of a monitor, intuition will keep you close to your target range.

Use more difficult gears

Keep your pedal cadence at 80–90 RPMs. Use slightly more difficult gearing— gears that would normally be too difficult build power. Think about finesse when pedaling a more difficult gear during power training. Finesse the pedals, don't mash them; think "circular" and "smooth." You'll be surprised at how difficult a gear you can maintain when you focus on being smooth and circular on your pedals. Shift to an easier gear if you find yourself struggling too much in a difficult gear, because it's better to be smooth and efficient in an easier gear than to mash a more difficult one.

Concentrate on power, not speed

Concentrate on building controlled power and momentum, not speed. Focus on tempo. Visualize your legs as a metronome: constant, smooth, and strong. Keep your effort and speed smooth and even through the difficult sections of your training course. Working harder for short periods to maintain your momentum is easier than attempting to regain it. That's power.

Add hills to your power rides

Use power rides in the hills to improve your hill climbing strength and endurance. As on flat and rolling terrain power rides: (1) target an 85%–95% effort range, (2) maintain a smooth pedal stroke, and (3) work a slightly tougher gear than normal. Use sections of hills for 15 to 45 minute power rides.

Ride flat and rolling power courses for several weeks before beginning hill power rides. Start with easier and work toward more difficult hills. Alternate riding positions between sitting and standing to prevent overworking one muscle group.

Sample power workouts

Refer to this sample week of of training incorporating power workouts:

Monday: *Medium distance ride*
Tuesday: *Power ride on flat terrain*
Wednesday: *Cycling day off*
Thursday: *Long ride*
Friday: *Cycling day off*
Saturday: *Power ride on rolling terrain*
Sunday: *Medium easy ride*

Refer to this sample week of of training incorporating hill power workouts:

Monday: *Medium distance ride*
Tuesday: *Power ride on flat terrain, with 15-30 minutes easy hills*
Wednesday: *Cycling day off*
Thursday: *Long ride*
Friday: *Cycling day off*
Saturday: *Power ride on rolling terrain, with 30-45 minutes hard hills*
Sunday: *Medium easy ride*

Intervals

Organize your workouts into repeated intervals that focus on developing speed. Use shorter intervals to help build speed for sprinting in break–aways, out of corners, or in sprint finishes. Concentrate on longer intervals to develop speed which can be used in time trials. Be sure to build a solid base of 4–6 weeks of cycling endurance training, and 2–4 weeks of cycling power training before incorporating any interval work.

Find a course for your intervals that is flat, slightly downhill, or mildly rolling. Do your intervals with a slight tail wind whenever possible, to help you develop speed, not power or strength.

Intervals

Design your intervals to last a minimum of two minutes and cover a maximum of 10 miles. Any longer and you'll be doing a power workout instead of speed work. Do fewer intervals as you increase their length. For example, you might do 10 x 2-minute intervals, or 2 x 10-mile intervals. Recover completely between intervals, with breathing controlled, heart resting and mind ready for another intense effort.

Interval workouts

Use these workouts to develop your speed:

2-minute/5-minute intervals

Use a 15–30 minute ride to your interval course as warm up. Ride all out for a 2-minute interval. Ride easy as you recover fully before your next interval. Repeat for a total of 4 x 2-minute intervals. Follow this set of intervals with a set of 2 x 5-minute intervals. Recover fully then do 2 x 2-minute intervals. Recover fully then do 2 x 5-minute intervals. Recover fully then do 1 x 5-minute interval. Cool down with a 15 minute easy ride to end workout.

Pyramid intervals

Use a 15–30 minute ride to your interval course as warm up. Ride all out for a 60-second interval. Follow with 60-seconds of recovery. Next ride all out for a 50-second interval, followed by a 50-second rest. Reduce the interval and rest times by 10-second jumps down to 20-second intervals. Recover completely after this set. Repeat set for a total of two-four sets. Cool down with a 15 minute easy ride to end workout.

On/Off intervals

Use a 15–30 minute ride to your interval course as warm up. Start from a medium speed. Then go all out for 15-seconds. Then coast for 15-seconds. Follow this with 15-seconds all out, with 15-seconds coast. Repeat eight–10 times per set. Repeat set up to four times. Cool down with a 15 minute easy ride to end workout.

5-minute/2-mile intervals

Use a 15–30 minute ride to your interval course as warm up. Ride all-out for a 5-minute interval. Ride easy between intervals to recover fully. Repeat for a total of 2 x 5-minute intervals. Follow this set with a set of 2-mile intervals. Ride easy between intervals to recover fully. Repeat for a 2 x 2-mile intervals. Cool down with 15 minute easy ride to end workout.

10-mile intervals

Use a 15–30 minute ride to your interval course as warm up. Ride 100% effort for a 10-mile interval. Concentrate on speed. Your slightly downhill course will help you maintain fast MPH and RPMs through the entire interval. Ride easy to recover fully. Repeat 10-mile interval for a total of 2 x 10-mile intervals. Cool down with 15 minute easy ride to end workout.

Sample week with intervals

Refer to this sample week of incorporating speed workouts (note focus on quality, not quantity):

Monday: *Medium distance endurance ride*
Tuesday: *Medium distance power ride on flat terrain*
Wednesday: *Day off*
Thursday: *5-minute/2-mile intervals*
Friday: *Day off*
Saturday: *2-minute/5-minute intervals*
Sunday: *10-mile intervals*

Fun Ones

Mix it up to stay fresh
Mix up your workouts to prevent boredom and injury. Here are ideas to keep your workouts interesting and fresh. Be creative. Have fun. That's what training's all about, isn't it?

Point-to-point rides
Do a course other than your usual one that starts and finishes at your house. Ride from point A to point B, and arrange a ride (other than your bike) back from point B to point A. Maybe pick a point B that offers huge breakfasts or lunches.

Scenic rides
Drive to the beach, lake front or mountains to find a scenic backdrop for a workout as good for your attitude as it is for your body.

Trail work
Find an off road trail away from the traffic and exhaust to do a mountain bike ride with burning uphills and screaming downhills.

Follow-the-leader
With one, two, or more, play follow-the-leader on a ride in whichever direction, at whatever speed, or up whatever hill the leader chooses.

Mini events
Set up mini-events with your training partners like circuits on lightly traveled roads around industrial parks, hill climbing challenges up your favorite painful hill, or destination challenges where breakfast goes to the winner.

Overtraining

Overtraining is the point where training and daily stresses combine to over-tax your system. A training program which may not be overtraining one week may be overtraining the next—because of additional stresses.

Be aware of possible overtraining as you: (1) increase your training level, or (2) experience a major changes or increases in your personal life.

Signs of overtraining
Watch for these signs of overtraining as you increase your training:

1) a higher than normal resting pulse-rate* when you first awaken,
2) trouble sleeping, or falling asleep,
3) feeling tired all the time, and
4) becoming upset more easily in every-day situations.

Cure overtraining
Back off your training if you think you may be overtraining:

1) take a couple of days off to give your body a chance to recover,
2) include at least 1–2 days per week of days-off or light workout days,
3) reduce the intensity of your training, like intervals, or very hard or long rides,
4) and get more rest, whether it's more sleep, or just more time when you're not always "on the go."

Trim your "training fat," and concentrate on quality not quantity because overtraining actually reduces your athletic performance levels. There's no reason to overtrain. So, train well, race well, have fun, and feel great.

To take your waking resting pulse rate, take your pulse at your neck or wrist when you first wake, before you get up out of bed. Track your waking resting pulse as you begin to increase training intensity and through your building and peak training to give you a norm against which you can compare future pulse rates.

Surviving Injuries

The joy of cycling can be matched in intensity only with the agony of an injury that prevents you from riding. Don't let the terrific progress you've made in your training program be derailed by an injury. Use these suggestions to (1) prevent injuries from hindering you in the first place, and (2) minimize the effect they have on your training and racing.

Prevention is the best cure

Clearly the best way to survive an injury is to avoid it in the first place. Avoid training injuries by following these reminders.

Stretch and warm up completely

Stretch before and after each ride. This is the simplest step you can take to prevent injury. Refer to the stretching tip in this guide for specific stretches to help you.

Ease into your rides. Design your training courses to allow you at least 2–5 miles of easy warm up before you settle into your workout's focused pace. This is the second simplest step to prevent injury. Just start out slowly!

Mix up your workouts

Most training injuries are caused by repeating too often the same workouts over and over again. Mix up your workouts: (1) Vary your distance; alternate short, medium and long rides into your training week. (2) Change your pace; ride easy on some days, medium on others and hard on some others depending on your workout focus. (3) Ride different courses to allow your body to build and recover; mix in rides that are flat, hilly, into-the-wind, with-the-wind, short or long. (4) Build your riding distance and intensity slowly over many weeks or months to give your body time to recover during building periods.

Cross-train

Cross-training is an extension of the idea of mixing up your workouts. Cross-training, instead of mixing-up your cycling workouts with other types of cycling workouts, mixes them with other sports: skiing, rowing, cross-country skiing, walking, swimming, or weightlifting.

Cross-train to help prevent running injuries by (1) giving your body a break from repeatedly doing the same movement, action and strain of cycling, and (2) by strengthening your body in ways that complement your cycling-developed muscles.

Minimize the damage after it's done

The goal is to try to prevent injuries. But if it's too late, here are some ideas to help you survive your training injury:

Find an acceptable way to rest

If it hurts when you ride, then you need to limit your cycling or stop entirely to give your body a chance to recuperate. To help survive this rest and limit your overall fitness loss, determine if all types of riding aggravate your injury, or only certain types (like hills or intervals). If it hurts only when you ride hills, then cut that out of your training. Or if medium or hard rides hurt, then try easy ones. This may help you retain sanity through your rest. Be aware of what training hurts you so you can avoid it before damage occurs.

If all cycling aggravates your injury, consider other training, such as swimming, rowing, cross-country skiing or weight-training. This should limit the overall loss of fitness during your recovery while giving your injury the time to heal.

Rest Earlier than Later

Whoever said "no pain, no gain" wasn't talking about getting ahead by pushing through an injury. Limit or eliminate the effect an injury has on your training by noticing and reacting to it early. Back off for a couple of days the quantity or intensity of your training if you notice a "slight" injury as you build your training program. Often a short rest, or reduction in training, at the first sign of an injury can save weeks of injury related problems down the road.

Ice, heat and elevation

When you're not entirely sidelined by your injury, you may be able to use ice and heat to let you continue training. Hold an ice pack against the spot of the injury immediately after working out to limit swelling from knee injuries, shin splints and ankle sprains. Use heat on the point of an injury to increase circulation to the area on injuries such as back sciatica. Elevate your injured limb to further reduce swelling.

Use your diary to identify the problem

Your training diary is often your most effective diagnostic tool to help you identify the cause of your injuries. Refer to your diary to see if an increase in distance or in strength or speed work precipitated your first injury symptoms. Look for a particular type of training distance, course or intensity that may have triggered your injury.

Use the diary to give you answers to your training and racing questions. Then, adjust your training to reduce, minimize or eliminate the problem.

Other Books to Read

This training guide offers tips to help you get more out of your training. Refer to these books for in-depth discussions of other training and racing topics:

Cycling
Berto, Frank, J: *Bicycle Magazine's Upgrading Your Bike*, Rodale Press
Borysewicz, Eddie: *Bicycle Road Racing*, Velo-News
Doughty, Tom: *The Complete Book of Long Distance and Competitive Cycling*, Simon & Schuster

Evan & Westell: *Cycle Racing*, Springfield Books
LeMond, Greg and Gordis, Kent: *Greg LeMond's Complete Book of Bicycling*, Putnam

Marino, John: *John Marino's Bicycling Book*, J.P. Tarcher
Sloane, E.: *Eugene A. Sloane's Bicycle Maintenance Manual*, Simon & Schuster
Van der Plas, Rob: *The Mountain Bike Book*, Bicycle Books

Cross-Training
Allen, Mark & Babbit, Bob: *Mark Allen's Total Triathlete*, Contempory Books
Fixx, James: *The Complete Book of Running*, Random House
Prins, Jan: *The Illustrated Swimmer*, Honolulu He'e
Scott, Dave & Barrett, Liz: *Dave Scott's Triathlon Training*, Simon & Schuster
Tinley, Scott: *Scott Tinley's Winning Triathlon*, Contempory Books
Vaz, K.: Cross Training, *The Complete Book of Triathlon*, Avon Publishers

Nutrition
Brody, Jane: *Jane Brody's Good Food Book*, Bantam Books
Haas, Robert: *Eat to Win*, Rawson Associate
The Complete & Up-to-Date Fat Book, a guide to the fat, calories and fat percentages in your food, Avery Publishing Group

Periodicals
Bicycling, 33 E. Minor Street, Emmaus, PA 18098
Bicycle Guide, 545 Boylston St., Boxton, MA 02116
Mountain Bike Action, 10600 Sepulveda Blvd., Mission Hills, CA 91345
Mountain Bike, Rodale Press, 33 E. Minor St., Emmaus, PA 18098
Mountain & City Biking, 7950 Deering Ave., Canoga Park, CA 91304
Triathlete, 1415 Third St., Suite 303, Santa Monica, CA 90401
Velo-News, 5595 Arapahoe Ave., Suite G, Boulder, CO 80303
Winning, 744 Roble Rd., Suite 190, Allentown, PA 18103

Getting More Out of Your Diary

Use your Cycle Log training diary as a tool to help you get more out of your training. The diary pages are simple and have extra room to write giving you the space and flexibility to decide what and how much information to record.

The diary can help keep you honest to your workout goals, like a personal coach does, by reminding you of what you have or haven't done. It can also provide a wealth of information to review to find out why you did well, or not-so-well in an event, or if you need to find the cause of an injury.

Use these suggestions (in addition to the course, distance and notes highlighted on the diary pages) as suggestions:

Note Days-Off

Draw a diagonal line through an entire day's diary section to show a day off from training. Days-off are critical to a good training program. But too many days-off will erode your training. Note why you took the day off, whether for rest, injury, or boredom. This will keep you honest or point to a need to change your schedule.

Adjust your notes to your changing needs throughout your season

Remember your Cycle Log diary allows you the flexibility to decide what training information is important *to you*, to record. This information may change through the year as you focus on different goals. For example, at the beginning of the year you may record your weight on a daily basis to help you focus on returning to your ideal training/race weight. While in mid-season you may note your weight only once a week and note your waking and resting pulse daily as you push your training toward overtraining.

Adjust your regular entries to your training goals and needs as they change throughout the season.

Note what you feel

How many miles and how many minutes you ride are important objective data to record each day. Equally important, and why Cycle Log is called a training diary, is the subjective data of how you feel during and after your training. Remember that day-to-day non-training demands (i.e. job, family or relationship stresses) impact your training as much as your workouts.

Take advantage of the extra space provided in this diary to note both training and non-training details which effect your overall training program. This subjective information can at times be more valuable than the objective numbers, like distance, or time in figuring why a particular program worked the way it did.

How to use charts

We've included four charts to help you better plan and track your training. Here's a summary of these charts and how to use them.

Goals Worksheet

Use this worksheet to list your goals at the beginning of your training program. Review your progress every one to three months to check your progress. Adjust your program as needed to meet your goals. Redefine your goals as your focus changes. And reward yourself for goals met.

Map to Raceday Worksheet

This worksheet will help you plan a multi-week training program for a specific event or race.

To plan your training for a specific event: (1) mark week #1 or #2 as your training peak for your event (1 or 2 weeks prior to the event); (2) mark the week number that you will begin your training; (3) plan each week's training in a schedule that will allow you to build gradually from your training starting point to your training peak. Never increase mileage more than 10% per week. Allow time to stay at "training plateaus" before moving on to subsequent stages of training.

Race Results Summary

The Race Results Summary lets you put all of your race results in one place. Remember to note any comments about the race or conditions that affected your results. Review this page against your training prior to races to learn what training works best for you.

Cumulative Mileage Chart

This chart lets you graph your training mileage. There are 28 vertical lines on two pages allowing you to graph 56 weeks (13 months) of training. Mark the week along the bottom of the chart and graph your weekly mileage to the corresponding distance level.

Goals Worksheet

Goal	Date Due	Date Completed	Comments

Map to Raceday Worksheet

	MON.	TUES.	WED.	THUR.	FRI.	SAT.	SUN.	REVIEW
WEEK #17	Type:___ Miles:___	Type:___ Miles:___	Type:___ Miles:___	Type:___ Miles:___	Type:___ Miles:___	Type:___ Miles:___	Type:___ Miles:___	Miles:___
WEEK #16	Type:___ Miles:___	Type:___ Miles:___	Type:___ Miles:___	Type:___ Miles:___	Type:___ Miles:___	Type:___ Miles:___	Type:___ Miles:___	Miles:___
WEEK #15	Type:___ Miles:___	Type:___ Miles:___	Type:___ Miles:___	Type:___ Miles:___	Type:___ Miles:___	Type:___ Miles:___	Type:___ Miles:___	Miles:___
WEEK #14	Type:___ Miles:___	Type:___ Miles:___	Type:___ Miles:___	Type:___ Miles:___	Type:___ Miles:___	Type:___ Miles:___	Type:___ Miles:___	Miles:___
WEEK #13	Type:___ Miles:___	Type:___ Miles:___	Type:___ Miles:___	Type:___ Miles:___	Type:___ Miles:___	Type:___ Miles:___	Type:___ Miles:___	Miles:___
WEEK #12	Type:___ Miles:___	Type:___ Miles:___	Type:___ Miles:___	Type:___ Miles:___	Type:___ Miles:___	Type:___ Miles:___	Type:___ Miles:___	Miles:___

Map to Raceday Worksheet

MON.	TUES.	WED.	THUR.	FRI.	SAT.	SUN.	REVIEW
WEEK #11 Type:____ Miles:____	Type:____ Miles:____	Type:____ Miles:____	Type:____ Miles:____	Type:____ Miles:____	Type:____ Miles:____	Type:____ Miles:____	Miles:____
WEEK #10 Type:____ Miles:____	Type:____ Miles:____	Type:____ Miles:____	Type:____ Miles:____	Type:____ Miles:____	Type:____ Miles:____	Type:____ Miles:____	Miles:____
WEEK #9 Type:____ Miles:____	Type:____ Miles:____	Type:____ Miles:____	Type:____ Miles:____	Type:____ Miles:____	Type:____ Miles:____	Type:____ Miles:____	Miles:____
WEEK #8 Type:____ Miles:____	Type:____ Miles:____	Type:____ Miles:____	Type:____ Miles:____	Type:____ Miles:____	Type:____ Miles:____	Type:____ Miles:____	Miles:____
WEEK #7 Type:____ Miles:____	Type:____ Miles:____	Type:____ Miles:____	Type:____ Miles:____	Type:____ Miles:____	Type:____ Miles:____	Type:____ Miles:____	Miles:____
WEEK #6 Type:____ Miles:____	Type:____ Miles:____	Type:____ Miles:____	Type:____ Miles:____	Type:____ Miles:____	Type:____ Miles:____	Type:____ Miles:____	Miles:____

Map to Raceday Worksheet

	MON.	TUES.	WED.	THUR.	FRI.	SAT.	SUN.	REVIEW
WEEK #5	Type:___ Miles:___	Type:___ Miles:___	Type:___ Miles:___	Type:___ Miles:___	Type:___ Miles:___	Type:___ Miles:___	Type:___ Miles:___	Miles:___
WEEK #4	Type:___ Miles:___	Type:___ Miles:___	Type:___ Miles:___	Type:___ Miles:___	Type:___ Miles:___	Type:___ Miles:___	Type:___ Miles:___	Miles:___
WEEK #3	Type:___ Miles:___	Type:___ Miles:___	Type:___ Miles:___	Type:___ Miles:___	Type:___ Miles:___	Type:___ Miles:___	Type:___ Miles:___	Miles:___
WEEK #2	Type:___ Miles:___	Type:___ Miles:___	Type:___ Miles:___	Type:___ Miles:___	Type:___ Miles:___	Type:___ Miles:___	Type:___ Miles:___	Miles:___
WEEK #1	Type:___ Miles:___	Type:___ Miles:___	Type:___ Miles:___	Type:___ Miles:___	Type:___ Miles:___	Type:___ Miles:___	Type:___ Miles:___	Miles:___
RACEWEEK	Type:___ Miles:___	Type:___ Miles:___	Type:___ Miles:___	Type:___ Miles:___	Type:___ Miles:___	Type:___ Miles:___	Type:___ Miles:___	Miles:___

Race Results Summary

Event	Course description and comments	Distance	Time	Avg. mph

Race Results Summary

Event	Course description and comments	Distance	Time	Avg. mph

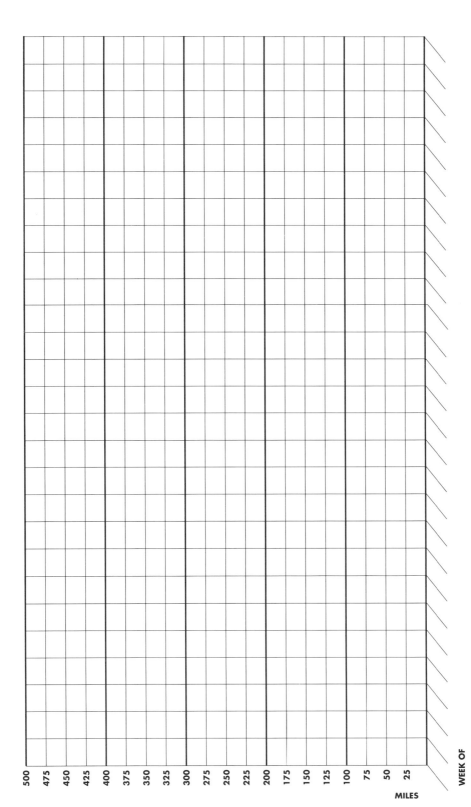

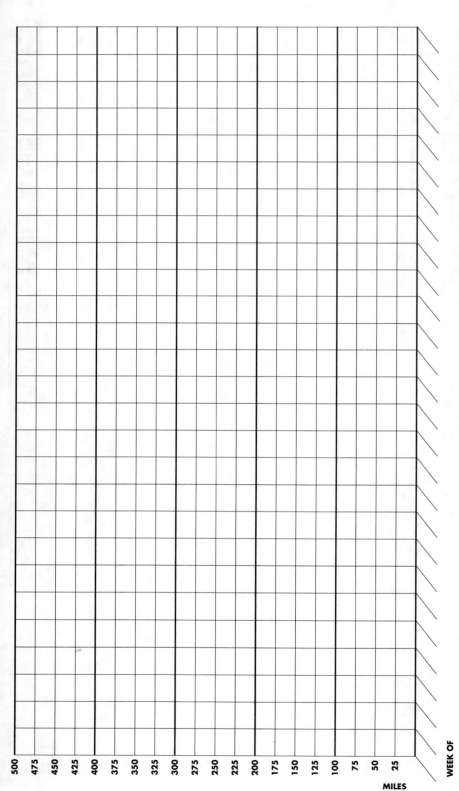

Previous page: Sunset Loop stage of the 1996 PowerBar Women's Challenge in Idaho. Above: Jan Eric Ostergaard in the 1997 Mt. St-Anne Cross Country, Quebec, Canada.

"Gray hair is God's graffiti."

— Bill Cosby

MON.

DATE _____

COURSE/NOTES _____

_____
_____
_____
_____
_____ MILES/TIME

TUES.

DATE _____

COURSE/NOTES _____

_____
_____
_____
_____
_____ MILES/TIME

WED.

DATE _____

COURSE/NOTES _____

_____
_____
_____
_____
_____ MILES/TIME

THUR.

DATE _____

COURSE/NOTES _____

_____
_____
_____
_____
_____ MILES/TIME

FRI.

DATE _____

COURSE/NOTES _____
_____
_____
_____
_____
_____ MILES/TIME

SAT.

DATE _____

COURSE/NOTES _____
_____
_____
_____
_____
_____ MILES/TIME

SUN.

DATE _____

COURSE/NOTES _____
_____
_____
_____
_____
_____ MILES/TIME

REVIEW

GOALS/NOTES _____
_____
_____
_____
_____

WEIGHT ____   CUMULATIVE TOTAL ____   WEEKLY TOTAL ____

MON.

DATE _____

COURSE/NOTES _____

_____
_____
_____
_____
_____
_____ MILES/TIME

TUES.

DATE _____

COURSE/NOTES _____

_____
_____
_____
_____
_____
_____ MILES/TIME

WED.

DATE _____

COURSE/NOTES _____

_____
_____
_____
_____
_____
_____ MILES/TIME

THUR.

DATE _____

COURSE/NOTES _____

_____
_____
_____
_____
_____
_____ MILES/TIME

DATE _____ **F**RI.

COURSE/NOTES _____
_____
_____
_____
_____
_____
_____ MILES/TIME [   ]

DATE _____ **S**AT.

COURSE/NOTES _____
_____
_____
_____
_____
_____
_____ MILES/TIME [   ]

DATE _____ **S**UN.

COURSE/NOTES _____
_____
_____
_____
_____
_____
_____ MILES/TIME [   ]

REVIEW

GOALS/NOTES _____
_____
_____
_____
_____
_____

WEIGHT [   ]   CUMULATIVE TOTAL [   ]   WEEKLY TOTAL [   ]

MON.

DATE _____

COURSE/NOTES _____
_____
_____
_____
_____
_____
_____ MILES/TIME [____]

TUES.

DATE _____

COURSE/NOTES _____
_____
_____
_____
_____
_____
_____ MILES/TIME [____]

WED.

DATE _____

COURSE/NOTES _____
_____
_____
_____
_____
_____
_____ MILES/TIME [____]

THUR.

DATE _____

COURSE/NOTES _____
_____
_____
_____
_____
_____
_____ MILES/TIME [____]

FRI.

DATE _____

COURSE/NOTES _____
_____
_____
_____
_____
_____
_____ MILES/TIME [   ]

SAT.

DATE _____

COURSE/NOTES _____
_____
_____
_____
_____
_____
_____ MILES/TIME [   ]

SUN.

DATE _____

COURSE/NOTES _____
_____
_____
_____
_____
_____
_____ MILES/TIME [   ]

REVIEW

GOALS/NOTES _____
_____
_____
_____
_____

WEIGHT [   ]   CUMULATIVE TOTAL [   ]   WEEKLY TOTAL [   ]

MON.

DATE _____

COURSE/NOTES _____
_____
_____
_____
_____
_____
_____
_____ MILES/TIME

TUES.

DATE _____

COURSE/NOTES _____
_____
_____
_____
_____
_____
_____
_____ MILES/TIME

WED.

DATE _____

COURSE/NOTES _____
_____
_____
_____
_____
_____
_____
_____ MILES/TIME

THUR.

DATE _____

COURSE/NOTES _____
_____
_____
_____
_____
_____
_____
_____ MILES/TIME

FRI.

DATE _____

COURSE/NOTES _____
_____
_____
_____
_____
_____
_____ MILES/TIME [   ]

SAT.

DATE _____

COURSE/NOTES _____
_____
_____
_____
_____
_____
_____ MILES/TIME [   ]

SUN.

DATE _____

COURSE/NOTES _____
_____
_____
_____
_____
_____
_____ MILES/TIME [   ]

REVIEW

GOALS/NOTES _____
_____
_____
_____
_____
_____

WEIGHT [   ]   CUMULATIVE TOTAL [   ]   WEEKLY TOTAL [   ]

MON.

DATE _____

COURSE/NOTES _____
_____
_____
_____
_____
_____ MILES/TIME

TUES.

DATE _____

COURSE/NOTES _____
_____
_____
_____
_____
_____ MILES/TIME

WED.

DATE _____

COURSE/NOTES _____
_____
_____
_____
_____
_____ MILES/TIME

THUR.

DATE _____

COURSE/NOTES _____
_____
_____
_____
_____
_____ MILES/TIME

FRI.

DATE _____

COURSE/NOTES _____
_____
_____
_____
_____
_____ MILES/TIME [____]

SAT.

DATE _____

COURSE/NOTES _____
_____
_____
_____
_____
_____ MILES/TIME [____]

SUN.

DATE _____

COURSE/NOTES _____
_____
_____
_____
_____
_____ MILES/TIME [____]

REVIEW

GOALS/NOTES _____
_____
_____
_____
_____

WEIGHT [____]   CUMULATIVE TOTAL [____]   WEEKLY TOTAL [____]

MON.

DATE _____

COURSE/NOTES _____
_____
_____
_____
_____
_____ MILES/TIME [   ]

TUES.

DATE _____

COURSE/NOTES _____
_____
_____
_____
_____
_____ MILES/TIME [   ]

WED.

DATE _____

COURSE/NOTES _____
_____
_____
_____
_____
_____ MILES/TIME [   ]

THUR.

DATE _____

COURSE/NOTES _____
_____
_____
_____
_____
_____ MILES/TIME [   ]

DATE _____

FRI.

COURSE/NOTES _____
_____
_____
_____
_____
_____
_____ MILES/TIME [   ]

DATE _____

SAT.

COURSE/NOTES _____
_____
_____
_____
_____
_____
_____ MILES/TIME [   ]

DATE _____

SUN.

COURSE/NOTES _____
_____
_____
_____
_____
_____
_____ MILES/TIME [   ]

REVIEW

GOALS/NOTES _____
_____
_____
_____
_____
_____

WEIGHT [   ]   CUMULATIVE TOTAL [   ]   WEEKLY TOTAL [   ]

MON.

DATE _____

COURSE/NOTES _____
_____
_____
_____
_____
_____
_____ MILES/TIME

TUES.

DATE _____

COURSE/NOTES _____
_____
_____
_____
_____
_____
_____ MILES/TIME

WED.

DATE _____

COURSE/NOTES _____
_____
_____
_____
_____
_____
_____ MILES/TIME

THUR.

DATE _____

COURSE/NOTES _____
_____
_____
_____
_____
_____
_____ MILES/TIME

FRI.

DATE _____

COURSE/NOTES _____
_____
_____
_____
_____
_____
_____ MILES/TIME

SAT.

DATE _____

COURSE/NOTES _____
_____
_____
_____
_____
_____
_____ MILES/TIME

SUN.

DATE _____

COURSE/NOTES _____
_____
_____
_____
_____
_____
_____ MILES/TIME

REVIEW

GOALS/NOTES _____
_____
_____
_____
_____
_____

WEIGHT   CUMULATIVE TOTAL   WEEKLY TOTAL

Above: US National Team, Team Cox Atlanta, in the 1997 Team Pursuit EDS Track Cup, San Diego, California. Right: Joe Lawwill, in the 1996 Mammoth Mountain NCS Kamikaze, Mammoth, California.

"A good man is always a beginner."

— Martial

The Peloton moves through the Provo, Utah, stage in the 1996 PowerBar Women's Challenge.

"You are no bigger than the things that annoy you."

— Jerry Bundsen

MON. DATE _____

COURSE/NOTES _____
_____
_____
_____
_____
_____ MILES/TIME [_____]

TUES. DATE _____

COURSE/NOTES _____
_____
_____
_____
_____
_____ MILES/TIME [_____]

WED. DATE _____

COURSE/NOTES _____
_____
_____
_____
_____
_____ MILES/TIME [_____]

THUR. DATE _____

COURSE/NOTES _____
_____
_____
_____
_____
_____ MILES/TIME [_____]

FRI.

DATE _____

COURSE/NOTES _____
_____
_____
_____
_____
_____
_____ MILES/TIME [____]

SAT.

DATE _____

COURSE/NOTES _____
_____
_____
_____
_____
_____
_____ MILES/TIME [____]

SUN.

DATE _____

COURSE/NOTES _____
_____
_____
_____
_____
_____
_____ MILES/TIME [____]

REVIEW

GOALS/NOTES _____
_____
_____
_____
_____
_____

WEIGHT [____]   CUMULATIVE TOTAL [____]   WEEKLY TOTAL [____]

MON.

DATE _____

COURSE/NOTES _____
_____
_____
_____
_____
_____
_____ MILES/TIME

TUES.

DATE _____

COURSE/NOTES _____
_____
_____
_____
_____
_____
_____ MILES/TIME

WED.

DATE _____

COURSE/NOTES _____
_____
_____
_____
_____
_____
_____ MILES/TIME

THUR.

DATE _____

COURSE/NOTES _____
_____
_____
_____
_____
_____
_____ MILES/TIME

FRI.

DATE _____

COURSE/NOTES _____
_____
_____
_____
_____
_____
_____ MILES/TIME

SAT.

DATE _____

COURSE/NOTES _____
_____
_____
_____
_____
_____
_____ MILES/TIME

SUN.

DATE _____

COURSE/NOTES _____
_____
_____
_____
_____
_____
_____ MILES/TIME

REVIEW

GOALS/NOTES _____
_____
_____
_____
_____
_____

WEIGHT _____   CUMULATIVE TOTAL _____   WEEKLY TOTAL _____

MON.   DATE _____

COURSE/NOTES _____
_____
_____
_____
_____
_____
_____ MILES/TIME [   ]

TUES.   DATE _____

COURSE/NOTES _____
_____
_____
_____
_____
_____
_____ MILES/TIME [   ]

WED.   DATE _____

COURSE/NOTES _____
_____
_____
_____
_____
_____
_____ MILES/TIME [   ]

THUR.   DATE _____

COURSE/NOTES _____
_____
_____
_____
_____
_____
_____ MILES/TIME [   ]

FRI.

DATE _____

COURSE/NOTES _____
_____
_____
_____
_____
_____ MILES/TIME

SAT.

DATE _____

COURSE/NOTES _____
_____
_____
_____
_____
_____ MILES/TIME

SUN.

DATE _____

COURSE/NOTES _____
_____
_____
_____
_____
_____ MILES/TIME

REVIEW

GOALS/NOTES _____
_____
_____
_____
_____

WEIGHT   CUMULATIVE TOTAL   WEEKLY TOTAL

MON.

DATE _____

COURSE/NOTES _____
_____
_____
_____
_____
_____
_____ MILES/TIME

TUES.

DATE _____

COURSE/NOTES _____
_____
_____
_____
_____
_____
_____ MILES/TIME

WED.

DATE _____

COURSE/NOTES _____
_____
_____
_____
_____
_____
_____ MILES/TIME

THUR.

DATE _____

COURSE/NOTES _____
_____
_____
_____
_____
_____
_____ MILES/TIME

DATE _____

FRI.

COURSE/NOTES _____
_____
_____
_____
_____
_____
_____ MILES/TIME [   ]

DATE _____

SAT.

COURSE/NOTES _____
_____
_____
_____
_____
_____
_____ MILES/TIME [   ]

DATE _____

SUN.

COURSE/NOTES _____
_____
_____
_____
_____
_____
_____ MILES/TIME [   ]

REVIEW

GOALS/NOTES _____
_____
_____
_____
_____
_____

WEIGHT [   ]   CUMULATIVE TOTAL [   ]   WEEKLY TOTAL [   ]

MON.

DATE _____

COURSE/NOTES _____
_____
_____
_____
_____
_____ MILES/TIME [   ]

TUES.

DATE _____

COURSE/NOTES _____
_____
_____
_____
_____
_____ MILES/TIME [   ]

WED.

DATE _____

COURSE/NOTES _____
_____
_____
_____
_____
_____ MILES/TIME [   ]

THUR.

DATE _____

COURSE/NOTES _____
_____
_____
_____
_____
_____ MILES/TIME [   ]

FRI.

DATE _____

COURSE/NOTES _____
_____
_____
_____
_____
_____
_____ MILES/TIME [   ]

SAT.

DATE _____

COURSE/NOTES _____
_____
_____
_____
_____
_____
_____ MILES/TIME [   ]

SUN.

DATE _____

COURSE/NOTES _____
_____
_____
_____
_____
_____
_____ MILES/TIME [   ]

REVIEW

GOALS/NOTES _____
_____
_____
_____
_____
_____

WEIGHT [   ]   CUMULATIVE TOTAL [   ]   WEEKLY TOTAL [   ]

MON.

DATE _____

COURSE/NOTES _____
_____
_____
_____
_____
_____
_____ MILES/TIME [____]

TUES.

DATE _____

COURSE/NOTES _____
_____
_____
_____
_____
_____
_____ MILES/TIME [____]

WED.

DATE _____

COURSE/NOTES _____
_____
_____
_____
_____
_____
_____ MILES/TIME [____]

THUR.

DATE _____

COURSE/NOTES _____
_____
_____
_____
_____
_____
_____ MILES/TIME [____]

FRI.

DATE _____

COURSE/NOTES _____
_____
_____
_____
_____
_____
_____ MILES/TIME

SAT.

DATE _____

COURSE/NOTES _____
_____
_____
_____
_____
_____
_____ MILES/TIME

SUN.

DATE _____

COURSE/NOTES _____
_____
_____
_____
_____
_____
_____ MILES/TIME

REVIEW

GOALS/NOTES _____
_____
_____
_____
_____

WEIGHT   CUMULATIVE TOTAL   WEEKLY TOTAL

MON.

DATE _____

COURSE/NOTES _____
_____
_____
_____
_____
_____
_____ MILES/TIME [___]

TUES.

DATE _____

COURSE/NOTES _____
_____
_____
_____
_____
_____
_____ MILES/TIME [___]

WED.

DATE _____

COURSE/NOTES _____
_____
_____
_____
_____
_____
_____ MILES/TIME [___]

THUR.

DATE _____

COURSE/NOTES _____
_____
_____
_____
_____
_____
_____ MILES/TIME [___]

DATE _____

FRI.

COURSE/NOTES _____

_____

_____

_____

_____

_____ MILES/TIME [   ]

DATE _____

SAT.

COURSE/NOTES _____

_____

_____

_____

_____

_____ MILES/TIME [   ]

DATE _____

SUN.

COURSE/NOTES _____

_____

_____

_____

_____

_____ MILES/TIME [   ]

REVIEW

GOALS/NOTES _____

_____

_____

_____

_____

WEIGHT [   ]   CUMULATIVE TOTAL [   ]   WEEKLY TOTAL [   ]

Above: Marcello Arrue on his way to winning the Match Sprint of the 1997 EDS Track Cup. Right: Carmen Richardson (yellow frame) and Susy Pryde in the Mountain Home Road Race of the 1996 PowerBar Women's Challenge, a 10 day stage race.

"Fanaticism consists of redoubling your efforts when you have forgotten your aim."

— *George Santayana*

Mark McCormick (front) and Bart Bowen in the '96 Tour du Pont, North Carolina.

"One hundred thousand lemmings can't be wrong."

— *Graffito*

MON.

DATE _____

COURSE/NOTES _____
_____
_____
_____
_____
_____
_____ MILES/TIME

TUES.

DATE _____

COURSE/NOTES _____
_____
_____
_____
_____
_____
_____ MILES/TIME

WED.

DATE _____

COURSE/NOTES _____
_____
_____
_____
_____
_____
_____ MILES/TIME

THUR.

DATE _____

COURSE/NOTES _____
_____
_____
_____
_____
_____
_____ MILES/TIME

FRI.

DATE _____

COURSE/NOTES _____
_____
_____
_____
_____
_____ MILES/TIME [   ]

SAT.

DATE _____

COURSE/NOTES _____
_____
_____
_____
_____
_____ MILES/TIME [   ]

SUN.

DATE _____

COURSE/NOTES _____
_____
_____
_____
_____
_____ MILES/TIME [   ]

REVIEW

GOALS/NOTES _____
_____
_____
_____
_____

WEIGHT [   ]   CUMULATIVE TOTAL [   ]   WEEKLY TOTAL [   ]

MON.   DATE _____

COURSE/NOTES _____
_____
_____
_____
_____
_____ MILES/TIME [   ]

TUES.   DATE _____

COURSE/NOTES _____
_____
_____
_____
_____
_____ MILES/TIME [   ]

WED.   DATE _____

COURSE/NOTES _____
_____
_____
_____
_____
_____ MILES/TIME [   ]

THUR.   DATE _____

COURSE/NOTES _____
_____
_____
_____
_____
_____ MILES/TIME [   ]

DATE _____

FRI.

COURSE/NOTES _____
_____
_____
_____
_____
_____
_____ MILES/TIME

DATE _____

SAT.

COURSE/NOTES _____
_____
_____
_____
_____
_____
_____ MILES/TIME

DATE _____

SUN.

COURSE/NOTES _____
_____
_____
_____
_____
_____
_____ MILES/TIME

REVIEW

GOALS/NOTES _____
_____
_____
_____
_____
_____

WEIGHT   CUMULATIVE TOTAL   WEEKLY TOTAL

MON.

DATE _____

COURSE/NOTES _____
_____
_____
_____
_____
_____
_____ MILES/TIME

TUES.

DATE _____

COURSE/NOTES _____
_____
_____
_____
_____
_____
_____ MILES/TIME

WED.

DATE _____

COURSE/NOTES _____
_____
_____
_____
_____
_____
_____ MILES/TIME

THUR.

DATE _____

COURSE/NOTES _____
_____
_____
_____
_____
_____
_____ MILES/TIME

FRI.

DATE _____

COURSE/NOTES _____
_____
_____
_____
_____
_____
_____ MILES/TIME [ ]

SAT.

DATE _____

COURSE/NOTES _____
_____
_____
_____
_____
_____
_____ MILES/TIME [ ]

SUN.

DATE _____

COURSE/NOTES _____
_____
_____
_____
_____
_____
_____ MILES/TIME [ ]

REVIEW

GOALS/NOTES _____
_____
_____
_____
_____
_____

WEIGHT [ ]   CUMULATIVE TOTAL [ ]   WEEKLY TOTAL [ ]

MON.

DATE _____

COURSE/NOTES _____
_____
_____
_____
_____
_____
_____ MILES/TIME

TUES.

DATE _____

COURSE/NOTES _____
_____
_____
_____
_____
_____
_____ MILES/TIME

WED.

DATE _____

COURSE/NOTES _____
_____
_____
_____
_____
_____
_____ MILES/TIME

THUR.

DATE _____

COURSE/NOTES _____
_____
_____
_____
_____
_____
_____ MILES/TIME

FRI.

DATE _____

COURSE/NOTES _____
_____
_____
_____
_____
_____
_____ MILES/TIME [ ]

SAT.

DATE _____

COURSE/NOTES _____
_____
_____
_____
_____
_____
_____ MILES/TIME [ ]

SUN.

DATE _____

COURSE/NOTES _____
_____
_____
_____
_____
_____
_____ MILES/TIME [ ]

REVIEW

GOALS/NOTES _____
_____
_____
_____
_____
_____

WEIGHT [ ]   CUMULATIVE TOTAL [ ]   WEEKLY TOTAL [ ]

MON. DATE _____

COURSE/NOTES _____
_____
_____
_____
_____
_____ MILES/TIME _____

TUES. DATE _____

COURSE/NOTES _____
_____
_____
_____
_____
_____ MILES/TIME _____

WED. DATE _____

COURSE/NOTES _____
_____
_____
_____
_____
_____ MILES/TIME _____

THUR. DATE _____

COURSE/NOTES _____
_____
_____
_____
_____
_____ MILES/TIME _____

DATE _____ **F**RI.

COURSE/NOTES _____
_____
_____
_____
_____
_____
_____ MILES/TIME

DATE _____ **S**AT.

COURSE/NOTES _____
_____
_____
_____
_____
_____
_____ MILES/TIME

DATE _____ **S**UN.

COURSE/NOTES _____
_____
_____
_____
_____
_____
_____ MILES/TIME

REVIEW

GOALS/NOTES _____
_____
_____
_____
_____
_____

WEIGHT   CUMULATIVE TOTAL   WEEKLY TOTAL

MON.

DATE _____

COURSE/NOTES _____
_____
_____
_____
_____
_____
_____ MILES/TIME

TUES.

DATE _____

COURSE/NOTES _____
_____
_____
_____
_____
_____
_____ MILES/TIME

WED.

DATE _____

COURSE/NOTES _____
_____
_____
_____
_____
_____
_____ MILES/TIME

THUR.

DATE _____

COURSE/NOTES _____
_____
_____
_____
_____
_____
_____ MILES/TIME

DATE _____   **F**RI.

COURSE/NOTES _____
_____
_____
_____
_____
_____
_____ MILES/TIME [   ]

DATE _____   **S**AT.

COURSE/NOTES _____
_____
_____
_____
_____
_____
_____ MILES/TIME [   ]

DATE _____   **S**UN.

COURSE/NOTES _____
_____
_____
_____
_____
_____
_____ MILES/TIME [   ]

REVIEW

GOALS/NOTES _____
_____
_____
_____
_____

WEIGHT [   ]   CUMULATIVE TOTAL [   ]   WEEKLY TOTAL [   ]

MON.

DATE _____

COURSE/NOTES _____
_____
_____
_____
_____
_____
_____ MILES/TIME

TUES.

DATE _____

COURSE/NOTES _____
_____
_____
_____
_____
_____
_____ MILES/TIME

WED.

DATE _____

COURSE/NOTES _____
_____
_____
_____
_____
_____
_____ MILES/TIME

THUR.

DATE _____

COURSE/NOTES _____
_____
_____
_____
_____
_____
_____ MILES/TIME

FRI.

DATE _____

COURSE/NOTES _____
_____
_____
_____
_____
_____
_____ MILES/TIME

SAT.

DATE _____

COURSE/NOTES _____
_____
_____
_____
_____
_____
_____ MILES/TIME

SUN.

DATE _____

COURSE/NOTES _____
_____
_____
_____
_____
_____
_____ MILES/TIME

REVIEW

GOALS/NOTES _____
_____
_____
_____
_____
_____

WEIGHT | CUMULATIVE TOTAL | WEEKLY TOTAL

Above: Rob Warner, of Great Britian, in the 1996 World Cup Downhill, Honolulu, Hawaii. Right: Nate Reiss, 1997 US Postal Service Team Member, in the 1997 Redlands Road Race, Redlands, California.

"Nice guys finish last, but we get to sleep in."

— Evan Davis

Dirk Copeland, Team Pursuit National Champion, in the 1997 Redlands Road Race.

"I always turn to the sports pages first, which record people's accomplishments. The front page has nothing but man's failures."

— *Chief Justice Earl Warren*

MON. DATE _____

COURSE/NOTES _____

_____
_____
_____
_____
_____
_____ MILES/TIME

TUES. DATE _____

COURSE/NOTES _____

_____
_____
_____
_____
_____
_____ MILES/TIME

WED. DATE _____

COURSE/NOTES _____

_____
_____
_____
_____
_____
_____ MILES/TIME

THUR. DATE _____

COURSE/NOTES _____

_____
_____
_____
_____
_____
_____ MILES/TIME

DATE _____ **F**RI.

COURSE/NOTES _____
_____
_____
_____
_____
_____ MILES/TIME [____]

DATE _____ **S**AT.

COURSE/NOTES _____
_____
_____
_____
_____
_____ MILES/TIME [____]

DATE _____ **S**UN.

COURSE/NOTES _____
_____
_____
_____
_____
_____ MILES/TIME [____]

REVIEW

GOALS/NOTES _____
_____
_____
_____
_____

WEIGHT [____]   CUMULATIVE TOTAL [____]   WEEKLY TOTAL [____]

MON.

DATE _____

COURSE/NOTES _____
_____
_____
_____
_____
_____ MILES/TIME [_____]

TUES.

DATE _____

COURSE/NOTES _____
_____
_____
_____
_____
_____ MILES/TIME [_____]

WED.

DATE _____

COURSE/NOTES _____
_____
_____
_____
_____
_____ MILES/TIME [_____]

THUR.

DATE _____

COURSE/NOTES _____
_____
_____
_____
_____
_____ MILES/TIME [_____]

FRI.

DATE _____

COURSE/NOTES _____
_____
_____
_____
_____
_____
_____ MILES/TIME

SAT.

DATE _____

COURSE/NOTES _____
_____
_____
_____
_____
_____
_____ MILES/TIME

SUN.

DATE _____

COURSE/NOTES _____
_____
_____
_____
_____
_____
_____ MILES/TIME

REVIEW

GOALS/NOTES _____
_____
_____
_____
_____
_____

WEIGHT ____   CUMULATIVE TOTAL ____   WEEKLY TOTAL ____

MON.

DATE _____

COURSE/NOTES _____
_____
_____
_____
_____
_____
_____ MILES/TIME

TUES.

DATE _____

COURSE/NOTES _____
_____
_____
_____
_____
_____
_____ MILES/TIME

WED.

DATE _____

COURSE/NOTES _____
_____
_____
_____
_____
_____
_____ MILES/TIME

THUR.

DATE _____

COURSE/NOTES _____
_____
_____
_____
_____
_____
_____ MILES/TIME

DATE _____ **F**RI.

COURSE/NOTES _____
_____
_____
_____
_____
_____
_____ MILES/TIME ☐

DATE _____ **S**AT.

COURSE/NOTES _____
_____
_____
_____
_____
_____
_____ MILES/TIME ☐

DATE _____ **S**UN.

COURSE/NOTES _____
_____
_____
_____
_____
_____
_____ MILES/TIME ☐

REVIEW

GOALS/NOTES _____
_____
_____
_____
_____
_____

WEIGHT ☐   CUMULATIVE TOTAL ☐   WEEKLY TOTAL ☐

MON.

DATE _____

COURSE/NOTES _____
_____
_____
_____
_____
_____
_____ MILES/TIME ____

TUES.

DATE _____

COURSE/NOTES _____
_____
_____
_____
_____
_____
_____ MILES/TIME ____

WED.

DATE _____

COURSE/NOTES _____
_____
_____
_____
_____
_____
_____ MILES/TIME ____

THUR.

DATE _____

COURSE/NOTES _____
_____
_____
_____
_____
_____
_____ MILES/TIME ____

FRI.

DATE _____

COURSE/NOTES _____
_____
_____
_____
_____
_____
_____ MILES/TIME

SAT.

DATE _____

COURSE/NOTES _____
_____
_____
_____
_____
_____
_____ MILES/TIME

SUN.

DATE _____

COURSE/NOTES _____
_____
_____
_____
_____
_____
_____ MILES/TIME

REVIEW

GOALS/NOTES _____
_____
_____
_____
_____

WEIGHT □   CUMULATIVE TOTAL □   WEEKLY TOTAL □

MON.

DATE _____

COURSE/NOTES _____
_____
_____
_____
_____
_____
_____ MILES/TIME [   ]

TUES.

DATE _____

COURSE/NOTES _____
_____
_____
_____
_____
_____
_____ MILES/TIME [   ]

WED.

DATE _____

COURSE/NOTES _____
_____
_____
_____
_____
_____
_____ MILES/TIME [   ]

THUR.

DATE _____

COURSE/NOTES _____
_____
_____
_____
_____
_____
_____ MILES/TIME [   ]

FRI.

DATE _____

COURSE/NOTES _____
_____
_____
_____
_____
_____ MILES/TIME _____

SAT.

DATE _____

COURSE/NOTES _____
_____
_____
_____
_____
_____ MILES/TIME _____

SUN.

DATE _____

COURSE/NOTES _____
_____
_____
_____
_____
_____ MILES/TIME _____

REVIEW

GOALS/NOTES _____
_____
_____
_____
_____

WEIGHT _____   CUMULATIVE TOTAL _____   WEEKLY TOTAL _____

MON.

DATE _____

COURSE/NOTES _____
_____
_____
_____
_____
_____
_____ MILES/TIME

TUES.

DATE _____

COURSE/NOTES _____
_____
_____
_____
_____
_____
_____ MILES/TIME

WED.

DATE _____

COURSE/NOTES _____
_____
_____
_____
_____
_____
_____ MILES/TIME

THUR.

DATE _____

COURSE/NOTES _____
_____
_____
_____
_____
_____
_____ MILES/TIME

FRI.

DATE _____

COURSE/NOTES _____
_____
_____
_____
_____
_____
_____ MILES/TIME [ ]

SAT.

DATE _____

COURSE/NOTES _____
_____
_____
_____
_____
_____
_____ MILES/TIME [ ]

SUN.

DATE _____

COURSE/NOTES _____
_____
_____
_____
_____
_____
_____ MILES/TIME [ ]

REVIEW

GOALS/NOTES _____
_____
_____
_____
_____

WEIGHT [ ]   CUMULATIVE TOTAL [ ]   WEEKLY TOTAL [ ]

MON.

DATE _____

COURSE/NOTES _____
_____
_____
_____
_____
_____
_____ MILES/TIME

TUES.

DATE _____

COURSE/NOTES _____
_____
_____
_____
_____
_____
_____ MILES/TIME

WED.

DATE _____

COURSE/NOTES _____
_____
_____
_____
_____
_____
_____ MILES/TIME

THUR.

DATE _____

COURSE/NOTES _____
_____
_____
_____
_____
_____
_____ MILES/TIME

DATE _____

FRI.

COURSE/NOTES _____
_____
_____
_____
_____
_____
_____ MILES/TIME

DATE _____

SAT.

COURSE/NOTES _____
_____
_____
_____
_____
_____
_____ MILES/TIME

DATE _____

SUN.

COURSE/NOTES _____
_____
_____
_____
_____
_____
_____ MILES/TIME

REVIEW

GOALS/NOTES _____
_____
_____
_____
_____
_____

WEIGHT | CUMULATIVE TOTAL | WEEKLY TOTAL

Above: Dede Demet, Team Saturn, in the 4-day, 5-stage, Redlands 97 Road Race, Redlands, California. Right: Susan DeMattai in the 1996 NCS Cross Country, Big Bear, California.

"God gives talent. Work transforms talent into genius."

— *Anna Pavlova*

The Peloton stretches out in the 1997 Redlands Road Race.

"But to look back all the time is boring. Excitement lies in tomorrow."

— *Natalia Makarova*

MON.

DATE _____

COURSE/NOTES _____
_____
_____
_____
_____
_____
_____ MILES/TIME

TUES.

DATE _____

COURSE/NOTES _____
_____
_____
_____
_____
_____
_____ MILES/TIME

WED.

DATE _____

COURSE/NOTES _____
_____
_____
_____
_____
_____
_____ MILES/TIME

THUR.

DATE _____

COURSE/NOTES _____
_____
_____
_____
_____
_____
_____ MILES/TIME

FRI.

DATE _____

COURSE/NOTES _____

_____
_____
_____
_____
_____
_____ MILES/TIME _____

SAT.

DATE _____

COURSE/NOTES _____

_____
_____
_____
_____
_____
_____ MILES/TIME _____

SUN.

DATE _____

COURSE/NOTES _____

_____
_____
_____
_____
_____
_____ MILES/TIME _____

REVIEW

GOALS/NOTES _____

_____
_____
_____
_____
_____

WEIGHT _____   CUMULATIVE TOTAL _____   WEEKLY TOTAL _____

MON.

DATE _____

COURSE/NOTES _____
_____
_____
_____
_____
_____
_____ MILES/TIME [   ]

TUES.

DATE _____

COURSE/NOTES _____
_____
_____
_____
_____
_____
_____ MILES/TIME [   ]

WED.

DATE _____

COURSE/NOTES _____
_____
_____
_____
_____
_____
_____ MILES/TIME [   ]

THUR.

DATE _____

COURSE/NOTES _____
_____
_____
_____
_____
_____
_____ MILES/TIME [   ]

DATE _____ **F**RI.

COURSE/NOTES _____
_____
_____
_____
_____
_____
_____ MILES/TIME [ ]

DATE _____ **S**AT.

COURSE/NOTES _____
_____
_____
_____
_____
_____
_____ MILES/TIME [ ]

DATE _____ **S**UN.

COURSE/NOTES _____
_____
_____
_____
_____
_____
_____ MILES/TIME [ ]

REVIEW

GOALS/NOTES _____
_____
_____
_____
_____

WEIGHT [ ]   CUMULATIVE TOTAL [ ]   WEEKLY TOTAL [ ]

MON.

DATE _____

COURSE/NOTES _____
_____
_____
_____
_____
_____
_____ MILES/TIME [_____]

TUES.

DATE _____

COURSE/NOTES _____
_____
_____
_____
_____
_____
_____ MILES/TIME [_____]

WED.

DATE _____

COURSE/NOTES _____
_____
_____
_____
_____
_____
_____ MILES/TIME [_____]

THUR.

DATE _____

COURSE/NOTES _____
_____
_____
_____
_____
_____
_____ MILES/TIME [_____]

FRI.

DATE _____

COURSE/NOTES _____
_____
_____
_____
_____
_____ MILES/TIME [____]

SAT.

DATE _____

COURSE/NOTES _____
_____
_____
_____
_____
_____ MILES/TIME [____]

SUN.

DATE _____

COURSE/NOTES _____
_____
_____
_____
_____
_____ MILES/TIME [____]

REVIEW

GOALS/NOTES _____
_____
_____
_____
_____

WEIGHT [____]   CUMULATIVE TOTAL [____]   WEEKLY TOTAL [____]

MON.

DATE _____

COURSE/NOTES _____

_____
_____
_____
_____

_____
_____ MILES/TIME

TUES.

DATE _____

COURSE/NOTES _____

_____
_____
_____
_____

_____
_____ MILES/TIME

WED.

DATE _____

COURSE/NOTES _____

_____
_____
_____
_____

_____
_____ MILES/TIME

THUR.

DATE _____

COURSE/NOTES _____

_____
_____
_____
_____

_____
_____ MILES/TIME

FRI.

DATE _____

COURSE/NOTES _____
_____
_____
_____
_____
_____ MILES/TIME [ ]

SAT.

DATE _____

COURSE/NOTES _____
_____
_____
_____
_____
_____ MILES/TIME [ ]

SUN.

DATE _____

COURSE/NOTES _____
_____
_____
_____
_____
_____ MILES/TIME [ ]

REVIEW

GOALS/NOTES _____
_____
_____
_____
_____
_____

WEIGHT [ ]   CUMULATIVE TOTAL [ ]   WEEKLY TOTAL [ ]

MON.   DATE _____

COURSE/NOTES _____
_____
_____
_____
_____
_____ MILES/TIME [_____]

TUES.   DATE _____

COURSE/NOTES _____
_____
_____
_____
_____
_____ MILES/TIME [_____]

WED.   DATE _____

COURSE/NOTES _____
_____
_____
_____
_____
_____ MILES/TIME [_____]

THUR.   DATE _____

COURSE/NOTES _____
_____
_____
_____
_____
_____ MILES/TIME [_____]

FRI.

DATE _____

COURSE/NOTES _____
_____
_____
_____
_____
_____
_____ MILES/TIME [____]

SAT.

DATE _____

COURSE/NOTES _____
_____
_____
_____
_____
_____
_____ MILES/TIME [____]

SUN.

DATE _____

COURSE/NOTES _____
_____
_____
_____
_____
_____
_____ MILES/TIME [____]

REVIEW

GOALS/NOTES _____
_____
_____
_____
_____

WEIGHT [____]   CUMULATIVE TOTAL [____]   WEEKLY TOTAL [____]

MON.

DATE _____

COURSE/NOTES _____
_____
_____
_____
_____
_____
_____ MILES/TIME

TUES.

DATE _____

COURSE/NOTES _____
_____
_____
_____
_____
_____
_____ MILES/TIME

WED.

DATE _____

COURSE/NOTES _____
_____
_____
_____
_____
_____
_____ MILES/TIME

THUR.

DATE _____

COURSE/NOTES _____
_____
_____
_____
_____
_____
_____ MILES/TIME

FRI.

DATE _____

COURSE/NOTES _____
_____
_____
_____
_____
_____
_____ MILES/TIME [ ]

SAT.

DATE _____

COURSE/NOTES _____
_____
_____
_____
_____
_____
_____ MILES/TIME [ ]

SUN.

DATE _____

COURSE/NOTES _____
_____
_____
_____
_____
_____
_____ MILES/TIME [ ]

REVIEW

GOALS/NOTES _____
_____
_____
_____
_____
_____

WEIGHT [ ]   CUMULATIVE TOTAL [ ]   WEEKLY TOTAL [ ]

MON.

DATE _____

COURSE/NOTES _____
_____
_____
_____
_____
_____
_____ MILES/TIME [   ]

TUES.

DATE _____

COURSE/NOTES _____
_____
_____
_____
_____
_____
_____ MILES/TIME [   ]

WED.

DATE _____

COURSE/NOTES _____
_____
_____
_____
_____
_____
_____ MILES/TIME [   ]

THUR.

DATE _____

COURSE/NOTES _____
_____
_____
_____
_____
_____
_____ MILES/TIME [   ]

DATE _____

FRI.

COURSE/NOTES _____
_____
_____
_____
_____
_____
_____ MILES/TIME [   ]

DATE _____

SAT.

COURSE/NOTES _____
_____
_____
_____
_____
_____
_____ MILES/TIME [   ]

DATE _____

SUN.

COURSE/NOTES _____
_____
_____
_____
_____
_____
_____ MILES/TIME [   ]

REVIEW

GOALS/NOTES _____
_____
_____
_____
_____

WEIGHT [   ]   CUMULATIVE TOTAL [   ]   WEEKLY TOTAL [   ]

Above: Thomas Frichknecht wins the 1996 World Cup, Hawaii. Right: Top finisher Susy Pryde in the 1997 Redlands road race.

"I like being unconventional."

— *Florence Griffith Joyner*

Rune Hoyadahl in the Kualoa Ranch Stage of the 1997 Hawaiian Mountain Tour.

"It's never too late to be what you might have been."

— *George Eliot*

MON.

DATE _____

COURSE/NOTES _____
_____
_____
_____
_____
_____
_____ MILES/TIME

TUES.

DATE _____

COURSE/NOTES _____
_____
_____
_____
_____
_____
_____ MILES/TIME

WED.

DATE _____

COURSE/NOTES _____
_____
_____
_____
_____
_____
_____ MILES/TIME

THUR.

DATE _____

COURSE/NOTES _____
_____
_____
_____
_____
_____
_____ MILES/TIME

DATE _____ **F**RI.

COURSE/NOTES _____
_____
_____
_____
_____
_____
_____ MILES/TIME

DATE _____ **S**AT.

COURSE/NOTES _____
_____
_____
_____
_____
_____
_____ MILES/TIME

DATE _____ **S**UN.

COURSE/NOTES _____
_____
_____
_____
_____
_____
_____ MILES/TIME

REVIEW

GOALS/NOTES _____
_____
_____
_____
_____
_____

WEIGHT | CUMULATIVE TOTAL | WEEKLY TOTAL

MON.

DATE _____

COURSE/NOTES _____
_____
_____
_____
_____
_____
_____ MILES/TIME [____]

TUES.

DATE _____

COURSE/NOTES _____
_____
_____
_____
_____
_____
_____ MILES/TIME [____]

WED.

DATE _____

COURSE/NOTES _____
_____
_____
_____
_____
_____
_____ MILES/TIME [____]

THUR.

DATE _____

COURSE/NOTES _____
_____
_____
_____
_____
_____
_____ MILES/TIME [____]

FRI.

DATE _____

COURSE/NOTES _____
_____
_____
_____
_____
_____
_____ MILES/TIME [   ]

SAT.

DATE _____

COURSE/NOTES _____
_____
_____
_____
_____
_____
_____ MILES/TIME [   ]

SUN.

DATE _____

COURSE/NOTES _____
_____
_____
_____
_____
_____
_____ MILES/TIME [   ]

REVIEW

GOALS/NOTES _____
_____
_____
_____
_____
_____

WEIGHT [   ]   CUMULATIVE TOTAL [   ]   WEEKLY TOTAL [   ]

MON.

DATE _____

COURSE/NOTES _____
_____
_____
_____
_____
_____
_____ MILES/TIME [   ]

TUES.

DATE _____

COURSE/NOTES _____
_____
_____
_____
_____
_____
_____ MILES/TIME [   ]

WED.

DATE _____

COURSE/NOTES _____
_____
_____
_____
_____
_____
_____ MILES/TIME [   ]

THUR.

DATE _____

COURSE/NOTES _____
_____
_____
_____
_____
_____
_____ MILES/TIME [   ]

DATE _____

FRI.

COURSE/NOTES _____

_____
_____
_____
_____
_____
_____ MILES/TIME [ ]

DATE _____

SAT.

COURSE/NOTES _____

_____
_____
_____
_____
_____
_____ MILES/TIME [ ]

DATE _____

SUN.

COURSE/NOTES _____

_____
_____
_____
_____
_____
_____ MILES/TIME [ ]

REVIEW

GOALS/NOTES _____

_____
_____
_____
_____
_____

WEIGHT [ ]   CUMULATIVE TOTAL [ ]   WEEKLY TOTAL [ ]

MON.

DATE _____

COURSE/NOTES _____
_____
_____
_____
_____
_____
_____ MILES/TIME [_____]

TUES.

DATE _____

COURSE/NOTES _____
_____
_____
_____
_____
_____
_____ MILES/TIME [_____]

WED.

DATE _____

COURSE/NOTES _____
_____
_____
_____
_____
_____
_____ MILES/TIME [_____]

THUR.

DATE _____

COURSE/NOTES _____
_____
_____
_____
_____
_____
_____ MILES/TIME [_____]

DATE _____

FRI.

COURSE/NOTES _____
_____
_____
_____
_____
_____
_____ MILES/TIME [   ]

DATE _____

SAT.

COURSE/NOTES _____
_____
_____
_____
_____
_____
_____ MILES/TIME [   ]

DATE _____

SUN.

COURSE/NOTES _____
_____
_____
_____
_____
_____
_____ MILES/TIME [   ]

REVIEW

GOALS/NOTES _____
_____
_____
_____
_____

WEIGHT [   ]   CUMULATIVE TOTAL [   ]   WEEKLY TOTAL [   ]

MON.

DATE _____

COURSE/NOTES _____
_____
_____
_____
_____
_____ MILES/TIME

TUES.

DATE _____

COURSE/NOTES _____
_____
_____
_____
_____
_____ MILES/TIME

WED.

DATE _____

COURSE/NOTES _____
_____
_____
_____
_____
_____ MILES/TIME

THUR.

DATE _____

COURSE/NOTES _____
_____
_____
_____
_____
_____ MILES/TIME

DATE _____ **F**RI.

COURSE/NOTES _____
_____
_____
_____
_____
_____
_____ MILES/TIME [   ]

DATE _____ **S**AT.

COURSE/NOTES _____
_____
_____
_____
_____
_____
_____ MILES/TIME [   ]

DATE _____ **S**UN.

COURSE/NOTES _____
_____
_____
_____
_____
_____
_____ MILES/TIME [   ]

REVIEW

GOALS/NOTES _____
_____
_____
_____
_____

WEIGHT [   ]   CUMULATIVE TOTAL [   ]   WEEKLY TOTAL [   ]

MON.

DATE _____

COURSE/NOTES _____
_____
_____
_____
_____
_____ MILES/TIME

TUES.

DATE _____

COURSE/NOTES _____
_____
_____
_____
_____
_____ MILES/TIME

WED.

DATE _____

COURSE/NOTES _____
_____
_____
_____
_____
_____ MILES/TIME

THUR.

DATE _____

COURSE/NOTES _____
_____
_____
_____
_____
_____ MILES/TIME

FRI.

DATE _____

COURSE/NOTES _____
_____
_____
_____
_____
_____
_____ MILES/TIME [____]

SAT.

DATE _____

COURSE/NOTES _____
_____
_____
_____
_____
_____
_____ MILES/TIME [____]

SUN.

DATE _____

COURSE/NOTES _____
_____
_____
_____
_____
_____
_____ MILES/TIME [____]

REVIEW

GOALS/NOTES _____
_____
_____
_____
_____
_____

WEIGHT [____]   CUMULATIVE TOTAL [____]   WEEKLY TOTAL [____]

MON.

DATE _____

COURSE/NOTES _____
_____
_____
_____
_____
_____
_____ MILES/TIME [   ]

TUES.

DATE _____

COURSE/NOTES _____
_____
_____
_____
_____
_____
_____ MILES/TIME [   ]

WED.

DATE _____

COURSE/NOTES _____
_____
_____
_____
_____
_____
_____ MILES/TIME [   ]

THUR.

DATE _____

COURSE/NOTES _____
_____
_____
_____
_____
_____
_____ MILES/TIME [   ]

DATE _____ **F**RI.

COURSE/NOTES _____
_____
_____
_____
_____
_____
_____ MILES/TIME [   ]

DATE _____ **S**AT.

COURSE/NOTES _____
_____
_____
_____
_____
_____
_____ MILES/TIME [   ]

DATE _____ **S**UN.

COURSE/NOTES _____
_____
_____
_____
_____
_____
_____ MILES/TIME [   ]

REVIEW

GOALS/NOTES _____
_____
_____
_____
_____
_____

WEIGHT [   ]   CUMULATIVE TOTAL [   ]   WEEKLY TOTAL [   ]

*Above: Don Myrah in the 1997 World Cup, Napa, California.
Right: Ryan White takes a spill in the 1997 Downhill Run of the
Dual Challenge at the Winter X-Games, Snow Summit, California.*

"Luck is the residue of design."

— Branch Rickey

Seth Pelusi in the Redlands 97.

"One thing I do suffer from is over-confidence. It's something I'm working on."

— George Foreman

MON.

DATE _____

COURSE/NOTES _____
_____
_____
_____
_____
_____
_____ MILES/TIME

TUES.

DATE _____

COURSE/NOTES _____
_____
_____
_____
_____
_____
_____ MILES/TIME

WED.

DATE _____

COURSE/NOTES _____
_____
_____
_____
_____
_____
_____ MILES/TIME

THUR.

DATE _____

COURSE/NOTES _____
_____
_____
_____
_____
_____
_____ MILES/TIME

DATE _____ **F**RI.

COURSE/NOTES _____
_____
_____
_____
_____
_____
_____ MILES/TIME [   ]

DATE _____ **S**AT.

COURSE/NOTES _____
_____
_____
_____
_____
_____
_____ MILES/TIME [   ]

DATE _____ **S**UN.

COURSE/NOTES _____
_____
_____
_____
_____
_____
_____ MILES/TIME [   ]

REVIEW

GOALS/NOTES _____
_____
_____
_____
_____
_____

WEIGHT [   ]   CUMULATIVE TOTAL [   ]   WEEKLY TOTAL [   ]

MON.

DATE _____

COURSE/NOTES _____
_____
_____
_____
_____
_____
_____ MILES/TIME [ ]

TUES.

DATE _____

COURSE/NOTES _____
_____
_____
_____
_____
_____
_____ MILES/TIME [ ]

WED.

DATE _____

COURSE/NOTES _____
_____
_____
_____
_____
_____
_____ MILES/TIME [ ]

THUR.

DATE _____

COURSE/NOTES _____
_____
_____
_____
_____
_____
_____ MILES/TIME [ ]

FRI.

DATE _____

COURSE/NOTES _____
_____
_____
_____
_____
_____ MILES/TIME [   ]

SAT.

DATE _____

COURSE/NOTES _____
_____
_____
_____
_____
_____ MILES/TIME [   ]

SUN.

DATE _____

COURSE/NOTES _____
_____
_____
_____
_____
_____ MILES/TIME [   ]

REVIEW

GOALS/NOTES _____
_____
_____
_____
_____

WEIGHT [   ]   CUMULATIVE TOTAL [   ]   WEEKLY TOTAL [   ]

MON.

DATE _____

COURSE/NOTES _____
_____
_____
_____
_____
_____
_____ MILES/TIME [   ]

TUES.

DATE _____

COURSE/NOTES _____
_____
_____
_____
_____
_____
_____ MILES/TIME [   ]

WED.

DATE _____

COURSE/NOTES _____
_____
_____
_____
_____
_____
_____ MILES/TIME [   ]

THUR.

DATE _____

COURSE/NOTES _____
_____
_____
_____
_____
_____
_____ MILES/TIME [   ]

FRI.

DATE _____

COURSE/NOTES _____
_____
_____
_____
_____
_____
_____ MILES/TIME

SAT.

DATE _____

COURSE/NOTES _____
_____
_____
_____
_____
_____
_____ MILES/TIME

SUN.

DATE _____

COURSE/NOTES _____
_____
_____
_____
_____
_____
_____ MILES/TIME

REVIEW

GOALS/NOTES _____
_____
_____
_____
_____
_____

WEIGHT   CUMULATIVE TOTAL   WEEKLY TOTAL

MON.

DATE _____

COURSE/NOTES _____
_____
_____
_____
_____
_____
_____ MILES/TIME [   ]

TUES.

DATE _____

COURSE/NOTES _____
_____
_____
_____
_____
_____
_____ MILES/TIME [   ]

WED.

DATE _____

COURSE/NOTES _____
_____
_____
_____
_____
_____
_____ MILES/TIME [   ]

THUR.

DATE _____

COURSE/NOTES _____
_____
_____
_____
_____
_____
_____ MILES/TIME [   ]

FRI.

DATE _____

COURSE/NOTES _____
_____
_____
_____
_____
_____ MILES/TIME [   ]

SAT.

DATE _____

COURSE/NOTES _____
_____
_____
_____
_____
_____ MILES/TIME [   ]

SUN.

DATE _____

COURSE/NOTES _____
_____
_____
_____
_____
_____ MILES/TIME [   ]

REVIEW

GOALS/NOTES _____
_____
_____
_____
_____

WEIGHT [   ]   CUMULATIVE TOTAL [   ]   WEEKLY TOTAL [   ]

MON.

DATE _____

COURSE/NOTES _____
_____
_____
_____
_____
_____
_____ MILES/TIME

TUES.

DATE _____

COURSE/NOTES _____
_____
_____
_____
_____
_____
_____ MILES/TIME

WED.

DATE _____

COURSE/NOTES _____
_____
_____
_____
_____
_____
_____ MILES/TIME

THUR.

DATE _____

COURSE/NOTES _____
_____
_____
_____
_____
_____
_____ MILES/TIME

DATE _____ **F**RI.

COURSE/NOTES _____
_____
_____
_____
_____
_____
_____ MILES/TIME [ ]

DATE _____ **S**AT.

COURSE/NOTES _____
_____
_____
_____
_____
_____
_____ MILES/TIME [ ]

DATE _____ **S**UN.

COURSE/NOTES _____
_____
_____
_____
_____
_____
_____ MILES/TIME [ ]

REVIEW

GOALS/NOTES _____
_____
_____
_____
_____
_____

WEIGHT [ ]   CUMULATIVE TOTAL [ ]   WEEKLY TOTAL [ ]

MON.

DATE _____

COURSE/NOTES _____
_____
_____
_____
_____
_____ MILES/TIME [ ]

TUES.

DATE _____

COURSE/NOTES _____
_____
_____
_____
_____
_____ MILES/TIME [ ]

WED.

DATE _____

COURSE/NOTES _____
_____
_____
_____
_____
_____ MILES/TIME [ ]

THUR.

DATE _____

COURSE/NOTES _____
_____
_____
_____
_____
_____ MILES/TIME [ ]

FRI.

DATE _____

COURSE/NOTES _____
_____
_____
_____
_____
_____
_____ MILES/TIME [   ]

SAT.

DATE _____

COURSE/NOTES _____
_____
_____
_____
_____
_____
_____ MILES/TIME [   ]

SUN.

DATE _____

COURSE/NOTES _____
_____
_____
_____
_____
_____
_____ MILES/TIME [   ]

REVIEW

GOALS/NOTES _____
_____
_____
_____
_____

WEIGHT [   ]   CUMULATIVE TOTAL [   ]   WEEKLY TOTAL [   ]

MON.

DATE _____

COURSE/NOTES _____
_____
_____
_____
_____
_____
_____ MILES/TIME _____

TUES.

DATE _____

COURSE/NOTES _____
_____
_____
_____
_____
_____
_____ MILES/TIME _____

WED.

DATE _____

COURSE/NOTES _____
_____
_____
_____
_____
_____
_____ MILES/TIME _____

THUR.

DATE _____

COURSE/NOTES _____
_____
_____
_____
_____
_____
_____ MILES/TIME _____

FRI.

DATE _____

COURSE/NOTES _____
_____
_____
_____
_____
_____ MILES/TIME [ ]

SAT.

DATE _____

COURSE/NOTES _____
_____
_____
_____
_____
_____ MILES/TIME [ ]

SUN.

DATE _____

COURSE/NOTES _____
_____
_____
_____
_____
_____ MILES/TIME [ ]

REVIEW

GOALS/NOTES _____
_____
_____
_____
_____

WEIGHT [ ]   CUMULATIVE TOTAL [ ]   WEEKLY TOTAL [ ]

Alex Merckx in the tough Beech Mountain stage of the 1996 Tour du Pont.

"When you win, nothing hurts."

— Joe Namath

A group is off their bikes on the way up a steep climb at the 1997 World Cup Cross Country, Napa, California.

"If I'm too strong for some people, that's their problem"

— *Glenda Jackson*

MON.

DATE _____

COURSE/NOTES _____
_____
_____
_____
_____
_____ MILES/TIME

TUES.

DATE _____

COURSE/NOTES _____
_____
_____
_____
_____
_____ MILES/TIME

WED.

DATE _____

COURSE/NOTES _____
_____
_____
_____
_____
_____ MILES/TIME

THUR.

DATE _____

COURSE/NOTES _____
_____
_____
_____
_____
_____ MILES/TIME

DATE _____ **F**RI.

COURSE/NOTES _____
_____
_____
_____
_____
_____
_____ MILES/TIME [   ]

DATE _____ **S**AT.

COURSE/NOTES _____
_____
_____
_____
_____
_____
_____ MILES/TIME [   ]

DATE _____ **S**UN.

COURSE/NOTES _____
_____
_____
_____
_____
_____
_____ MILES/TIME [   ]

REVIEW

GOALS/NOTES _____
_____
_____
_____
_____
_____

WEIGHT [   ]   CUMULATIVE TOTAL [   ]   WEEKLY TOTAL [   ]

MON.

DATE _____

COURSE/NOTES _____
_____
_____
_____
_____
_____
_____ MILES/TIME

TUES.

DATE _____

COURSE/NOTES _____
_____
_____
_____
_____
_____
_____ MILES/TIME

WED.

DATE _____

COURSE/NOTES _____
_____
_____
_____
_____
_____
_____ MILES/TIME

THUR.

DATE _____

COURSE/NOTES _____
_____
_____
_____
_____
_____
_____ MILES/TIME

DATE _____ **F**RI.

COURSE/NOTES _____
_____
_____
_____
_____
_____
_____ MILES/TIME [   ]

DATE _____ **S**AT.

COURSE/NOTES _____
_____
_____
_____
_____
_____
_____ MILES/TIME [   ]

DATE _____ **S**UN.

COURSE/NOTES _____
_____
_____
_____
_____
_____
_____ MILES/TIME [   ]

REVIEW

GOALS/NOTES _____
_____
_____
_____
_____
_____

WEIGHT [   ]   CUMULATIVE TOTAL [   ]   WEEKLY TOTAL [   ]

MON.

DATE _____

COURSE/NOTES _____
_____
_____
_____
_____
_____
_____ MILES/TIME [_____]

TUES.

DATE _____

COURSE/NOTES _____
_____
_____
_____
_____
_____
_____ MILES/TIME [_____]

WED.

DATE _____

COURSE/NOTES _____
_____
_____
_____
_____
_____
_____ MILES/TIME [_____]

THUR.

DATE _____

COURSE/NOTES _____
_____
_____
_____
_____
_____
_____ MILES/TIME [_____]

DATE _____

COURSE/NOTES _____

_____
_____
_____
_____
_____
_____ MILES/TIME

FRI.

DATE _____

COURSE/NOTES _____

_____
_____
_____
_____
_____
_____ MILES/TIME

SAT.

DATE _____

COURSE/NOTES _____

_____
_____
_____
_____
_____
_____ MILES/TIME

SUN.

REVIEW

GOALS/NOTES _____

_____
_____
_____
_____
_____

WEIGHT | CUMULATIVE TOTAL | WEEKLY TOTAL

MON.

DATE _____

COURSE/NOTES _____
_____
_____
_____
_____
_____ MILES/TIME

TUES.

DATE _____

COURSE/NOTES _____
_____
_____
_____
_____
_____ MILES/TIME

WED.

DATE _____

COURSE/NOTES _____
_____
_____
_____
_____
_____ MILES/TIME

THUR.

DATE _____

COURSE/NOTES _____
_____
_____
_____
_____
_____ MILES/TIME

DATE _____

FRI.

COURSE/NOTES _____
_____
_____
_____
_____
_____
_____ MILES/TIME [   ]

DATE _____

SAT.

COURSE/NOTES _____
_____
_____
_____
_____
_____
_____ MILES/TIME [   ]

DATE _____

SUN.

COURSE/NOTES _____
_____
_____
_____
_____
_____
_____ MILES/TIME [   ]

REVIEW

GOALS/NOTES _____
_____
_____
_____
_____
_____

WEIGHT [   ]   CUMULATIVE TOTAL [   ]   WEEKLY TOTAL [   ]

MON.

DATE _____

COURSE/NOTES _____
_____
_____
_____
_____
_____
_____ MILES/TIME

TUES.

DATE _____

COURSE/NOTES _____
_____
_____
_____
_____
_____
_____ MILES/TIME

WED.

DATE _____

COURSE/NOTES _____
_____
_____
_____
_____
_____
_____ MILES/TIME

THUR.

DATE _____

COURSE/NOTES _____
_____
_____
_____
_____
_____
_____ MILES/TIME

DATE _____ **F**RI.

COURSE/NOTES _____
_____
_____
_____
_____
_____
_____ MILES/TIME [ ]

DATE _____ **S**AT.

COURSE/NOTES _____
_____
_____
_____
_____
_____
_____ MILES/TIME [ ]

DATE _____ **S**UN.

COURSE/NOTES _____
_____
_____
_____
_____
_____
_____ MILES/TIME [ ]

REVIEW

GOALS/NOTES _____
_____
_____
_____
_____

WEIGHT [ ]   CUMULATIVE TOTAL [ ]   WEEKLY TOTAL [ ]

MON.

DATE _____

COURSE/NOTES _____
_____
_____
_____
_____
_____ MILES/TIME

TUES.

DATE _____

COURSE/NOTES _____
_____
_____
_____
_____
_____ MILES/TIME

WED.

DATE _____

COURSE/NOTES _____
_____
_____
_____
_____
_____ MILES/TIME

THUR.

DATE _____

COURSE/NOTES _____
_____
_____
_____
_____
_____ MILES/TIME

FRI.

DATE _____

COURSE/NOTES _____
_____
_____
_____
_____
_____
_____ MILES/TIME [____]

SAT.

DATE _____

COURSE/NOTES _____
_____
_____
_____
_____
_____
_____ MILES/TIME [____]

SUN.

DATE _____

COURSE/NOTES _____
_____
_____
_____
_____
_____
_____ MILES/TIME [____]

REVIEW

GOALS/NOTES _____
_____
_____
_____
_____
_____

WEIGHT [____]   CUMULATIVE TOTAL [____]   WEEKLY TOTAL [____]

MON.

DATE _____

COURSE/NOTES _____
_____
_____
_____
_____
_____
_____ MILES/TIME [   ]

TUES.

DATE _____

COURSE/NOTES _____
_____
_____
_____
_____
_____
_____ MILES/TIME [   ]

WED.

DATE _____

COURSE/NOTES _____
_____
_____
_____
_____
_____
_____ MILES/TIME [   ]

THUR.

DATE _____

COURSE/NOTES _____
_____
_____
_____
_____
_____
_____ MILES/TIME [   ]

DATE _____ **F**RI.

COURSE/NOTES _____
_____
_____
_____
_____
_____
_____ MILES/TIME [   ]

DATE _____ **S**AT.

COURSE/NOTES _____
_____
_____
_____
_____
_____
_____ MILES/TIME [   ]

DATE _____ **S**UN.

COURSE/NOTES _____
_____
_____
_____
_____
_____
_____ MILES/TIME [   ]

REVIEW

GOALS/NOTES _____
_____
_____
_____
_____
_____

WEIGHT [   ]   CUMULATIVE TOTAL [   ]   WEEKLY TOTAL [   ]

Above: Australian Anna Wilson won the 1996 PowerBar Women's Challenge. Right: Olympic Gold Medalist Paola Pezzo on his way to winning the 1997 Mt. St-Anne World Cup Cross Country.

"If you don't play to win, why keep score?"

— *Vernon Law*